MODERN WEAPONS
COMPARED AND CONTRASTED

SMALL ARMS

MARTIN J. DOUGHERTY

rosen publishing's
rosen central

New York

This edition first published in 2013 by:

The Rosen Publishing Group, Inc.
29 East 21st Street
New York, NY 10010

Library of Congress Cataloging-in-Publication Data

Dougherty, Martin J.
Small arms/Martin J. Dougherty.
    p. cm.—(Modern weapons: compared and contrasted)
Includes bibliographical references and index.
ISBN 978-1-4488-9245-7 (library binding)
1. Firearms. 2. Military weapons. I. Title.
UD380.D69 2013
623.4'4—dc23

2012034788

Manufactured in the United States of America

CPSIA Compliance Information: Batch #W13YA: For further information, contact Rosen Publishing, New York, New York, at 1-800-237-9932.

Copyright © 2012 by Amber Books Ltd. First published in 2012 by Amber Books Ltd.

Contents

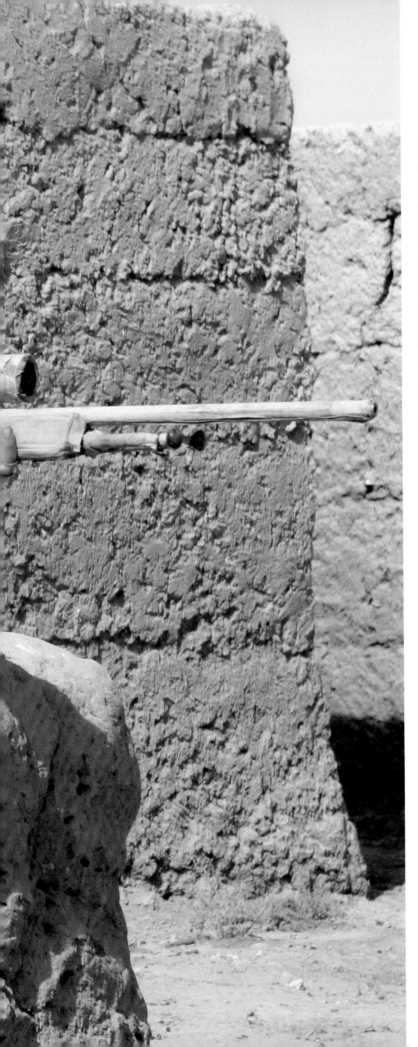

Introduction

Despite all the air power, armored vehicles and artillery support that can be brought to bear, it is the infantry that must take and hold ground, and for this task they need a variety of weapons. The term "small arms" originally referred to any firearms that were smaller than a cannon, but today it applies to individual weapons and some light support systems. The term is sometimes loosely used to include all the weapons systems carried and employed by infantry, including anti-armor and anti-aircraft weapons.

The assault rifle is the principal small arm on the modern battlefield, but an infantry force also needs support weapons and specialist systems such as long-range sniper rifles. For certain tasks, such as close-assault operations, security and urban combat, other weapons such as combat shotguns or submachine guns are a solid choice. A properly equipped force will be armed with a mix of all-round weapons systems to deal with most situations that might arise, supplemented by specialist weapons in the hands of suitably trained personnel.

LEFT: A British Army sniper team carries out overwatch duties somewhere in Afghanistan, 2009. The sniper is armed with an Accuracy International L96 rifle, which has been covered with non-reflective material to stop the barrel and other surfaces from giving away their position.

CHAPTER 1

Side Arms

Caliber and Magazine Capacity

- ▶ **SIG P226**
- ▶ **Browning 9mm L9A1**
- ▶ **PMM**
- ▶ **Heckler & Koch USP**
- ▶ **FN Five-Seven**

Handguns are issued in the military as back-up weapons, or where a measure of self-defense capability might be necessary but there is no space for a larger and more effective weapon. They are carried by officers, pilots, vehicle crews and other specialists who will only have to use their weapons when something has gone badly wrong.

Military semiautomatic pistols normally have a high magazine capacity. Handgun ammunition lacks stopping power and the weapon itself is far from accurate, so volume of fire can be critical. Early semiautomatics such as the Browning L9A1 and Makarov (PM/PMM), with a modest magazine capacity by today's standards, still offered an immense increase in firepower over revolvers.

Since the introduction of these weapons, handgun technology has steadily improved. The high-capacity SIG P226 is prized for its accuracy and reliability, while the USP returned to a traditional 11.4mm (0.45in) cartridge for improved stopping power, though at the price of reduced capacity. The Five-Seven uses a revolutionary small-caliber round with similar ballistics but improved penetrating power compared with the 9mm (0.35in) round. This gives even a handgun some chance to penetrate body armor or light cover.

Caliber

The stopping power of a handgun round depends on its mass and velocity. As a rule, a big round will put the target down more reliably than a smaller one. Many handgun users still swear by the 11.4mm (0.45in) round.

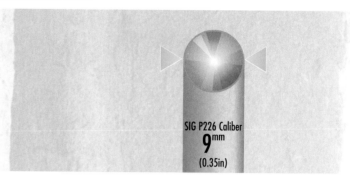

SIG P226 Caliber
9mm
(0.35in)

Browning 9mm L9A1 Caliber
9mm
(0.35in)

BELOW: The Sig Sauer P226 is a classic service pistol produced in Switzerland and used by numerous army and police forces throughout the world. The handgun chambers the powerful 9mm (0.35in) Parabellum round.

PMM Caliber
9mm
(0.35in)

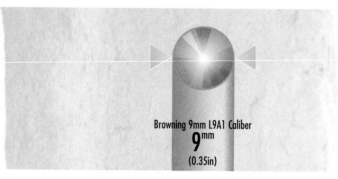

H&K USP Caliber
11.4mm
(0.45in)

FN Five-Seven Caliber
5.7mm
(0.224in)

Magazine Capacity

Magazine capacity is determined by the size of the magazine and the caliber of the rounds that go in it. Many modern handguns use a double-stacking system that increases capacity at the cost of a chunkier weapon. There is a limit to how wide a handgun grip can be before it becomes unusable.

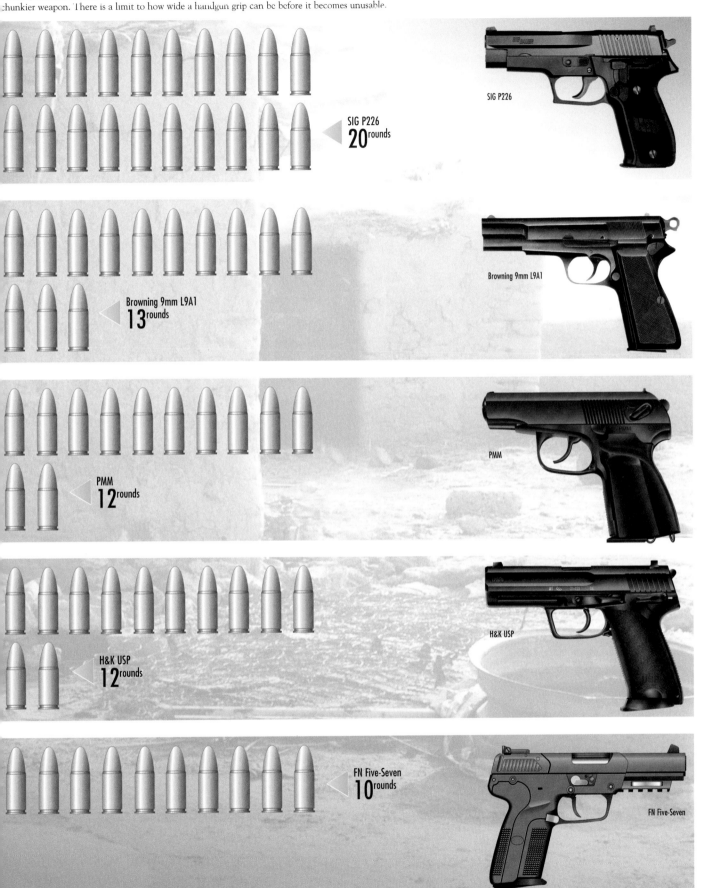

SIG P226

SIG P226
20 rounds

Browning 9mm L9A1

Browning 9mm L9A1
13 rounds

PMM

PMM
12 rounds

H&K USP

H&K USP
12 rounds

FN Five-Seven

FN Five-Seven
10 rounds

FN Five-Seven

7

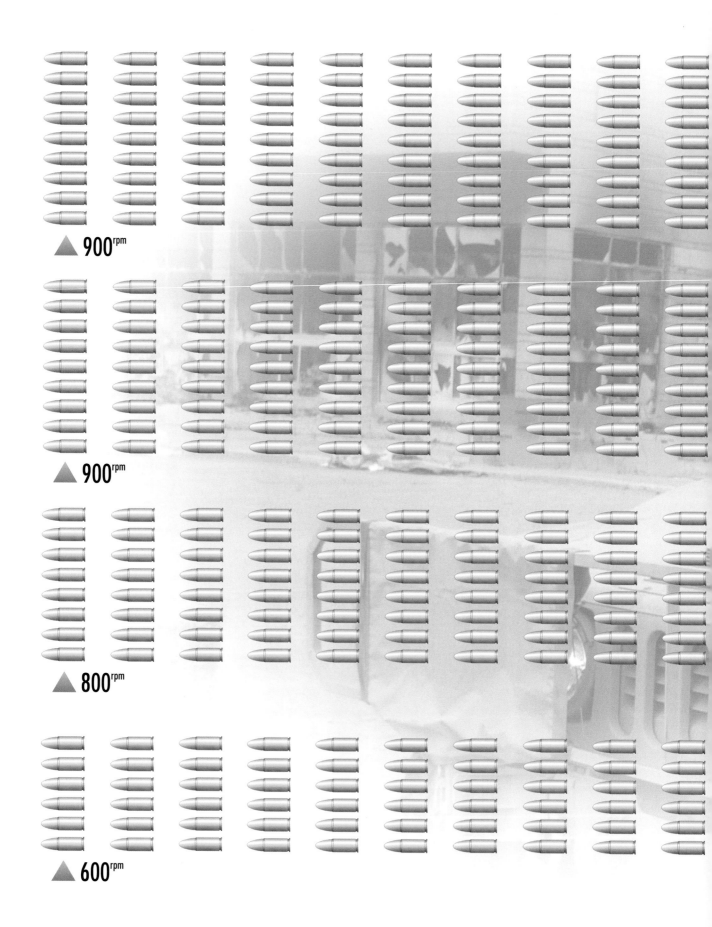

900rpm

900rpm

800rpm

600rpm

CHAPTER 2

Personal Defense Weapons 1

Rate of Fire

▶ **Heckler & Koch MP5K**
▶ **Agram 2000**
▶ **Ruger MP-9**
▶ **Steyr TMP**

Steyr TMP

H&K MP5K

Agram 2000

Ruger MP-9

The concept of a personal defense weapon is not new. Traditionally, artillery and vehicle crews, engineers and other personnel whose duties do not normally involve direct combat with the enemy were issued a carbine, submachine gun or handgun for self-defense. The modern personal defense weapon (PDW) has the same characteristics as these weapons, i.e. small size and light weight compared with a rifle, but is custom designed to offer an excellent combination of firepower and compactness.

Many PDWs are essentially small submachine guns, and fire handgun-caliber ammunition. The "industry standard" for most PDWs is 9mm (0.35in) Parabellum, offering a reasonable compromise between stopping power and capacity. Although a PDW's effective range is longer than that of a handgun, it is still short. This is perfectly acceptable – PDWs are intended for self-defense in an emergency, not as standard-issue combat weapons. Intense close-range firepower enables the user to deal with the immediate problem and then seek reinforcements or withdraw from the threat, so rate of fire and magazine capacity are more important than long-range accuracy.

A common feature on many PDWs is some kind of foregrip, which makes a weapon far more controllable in automatic-fire mode. The greater the distance between the user's hands, the more stable the weapon will be, even if it is being used without a shoulder stock. Although most PDWs can be fired one-handed, recoil tends to spray bullets around without a solid two-handed grip, and with a high rate of fire the weapon can be out of ammunition before the user brings it back on target.

Rate of Fire

In most situations where a PDW becomes necessary, the most effective course of action is to pour fire into the threat and withdraw rapidly. Close-range firefights tend to be brutally short, and victory will often go to whoever can get the most rounds downrange the fastest.

CHAPTER 3

Personal Defense Weapons 2

Effective Range

▶ **Heckler & Koch MP7**
▶ **Heckler & Koch UMP**
▶ **Steyr TMP**
▶ **Kinetics CPW**
▶ **FN P90**

H&K MP7

H&K UMP

Steyr TMP

Kinetics CPW

FN P90

The term "personal defense weapon" describes a role rather than a precise weapon design, and approaches to the concept vary considerably. Many PDWs are very small submachine guns, incorporating heavy firepower into a package little larger than a handgun. Others are larger, up to the size of a traditional submachine gun, and generally have a longer effective range. These types to some extent define the two main PDW concepts – either more potent but not much bigger than a handgun, or somewhat smaller but not hugely less effective (at least at short range) than a rifle.

Effective range is the product of various complex factors including muzzle velocity and barrel length. These largely determine the inherent accuracy of the weapon, but ergonomic factors are arguably more important. It does not matter so much how accurate a PDW is as how reliably its user can get it on target. A shoulder stock aids considerably in longer-range shooting, as does a longer barrel. The general layout of the weapon is also a critical factor: a well-designed weapon is instinctive to aim, which greatly improves effectiveness in short-range point-and-shoot engagements.

The smaller PDWs have a fairly short effective range, not least because they lack the mass to absorb recoil and thus suffer from muzzle climb under automatic fire. The MP7 suffers less from recoil effects due to its specialist 4.6x30mm (0.18x1.2in) ammunition, which produces relatively little recoil and offers both improved penetration and a much higher muzzle velocity than the standard pistol rounds used by many PDWs.

A handgun is better than nothing if a sudden threat emerges, whereas a PDW is much better than nothing. It is still not a battlefield weapon, however, and cannot replace an assault rifle except in security-related tasks and perhaps urban combat.

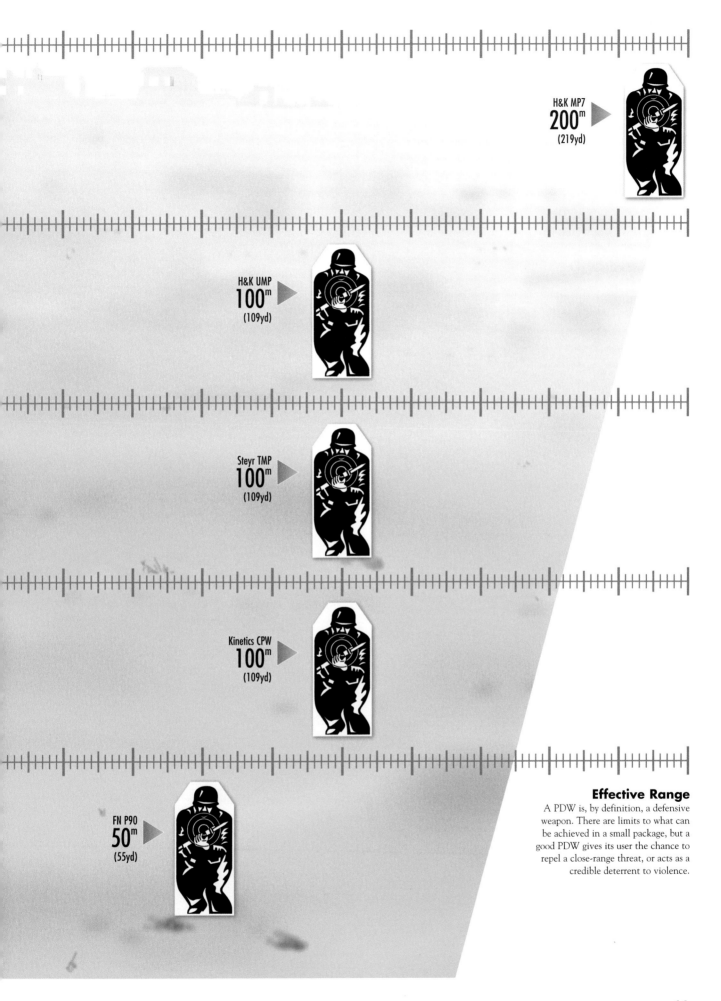

H&K MP7
200^m
(219yd)

H&K UMP
100^m
(109yd)

Steyr TMP
100^m
(109yd)

Kinetics CPW
100^m
(109yd)

FN P90
50^m
(55yd)

Effective Range

A PDW is, by definition, a defensive weapon. There are limits to what can be achieved in a small package, but a good PDW gives its user the chance to repel a close-range threat, or acts as a credible deterrent to violence.

CHAPTER 4

Close Assault Weapons 1

Effective Range and Magazine Capacity

▶ **Heckler & Koch MP5**
▶ **CZW 438 M9**
▶ **USAS-12**
▶ **Benelli M4/M1014**

For the close assault role, the weapons of choice are shotguns and light automatic weapons such as submachine guns. An assault weapon needs to be easily maneuvered in tight spaces and must be able to lay down heavy firepower to disable any threat quickly. At such a close range, an enemy that manages to shoot back has a good chance of inflicting casualties, so all hostiles need to be taken out of the fight quickly. A burst of pistol-caliber rounds or a shell filled with heavy buckshot will accomplish the task with great effectiveness.

Shotguns such as the semiautomatic M1014 are capable of fairly rapid fire, and each shell has good knockdown power against unarmored opponents. Shotguns are also useful for breaching doors, but they lack effectiveness against body armor and may not be able to engage multiple targets. Fully automatic shotguns, such as the USAS-12, can do so, and have a large magazine capacity to facilitate automatic fire.

Even so, drums are bulky and more traditional shotguns must be reloaded one shell at a time. Great precision is not necessary using standard shotgun ammunition, and the spread of shot does mean that a hit is likely even with a very hasty attempt. However, shot loses energy fast and becomes ineffective at ranges where a bullet would still be highly lethal.

Submachine guns and fully automatic personal defense weapons offer good firepower and can engage at somewhat longer ranges than shotguns. This is not significant when fighting through a building, but can be critical in a more open environment. Traditional submachine guns typically use 9mm (0.35in) ammunition, against which most body armor is effective.

OPPOSITE, TOP: US Navy SEALs train using H&K MP5 light assault weapons. The H&K MP5 is popular with special forces and police units.

Effective Range

Close combat requires light, short, handy weapons with high firepower, allowing a rapid and devastating response to any threat. An engagement at over 50m (55yd) is unlikely under most circumstances, making both shotguns and light automatic weapons good choices.

H&K MP5 Range **200ᵐ** (219yd)

CZW 438 M9 Range **200ᵐ** (219yd)

H&K MP5

CZW 438 M9

32 rounds

30 rounds

USAS-12 Range
200ᵐ
(219yd)

Benelli M4/M1014 Range
100ᵐ
(109yd)

USAS-12

20 rounds

Benelli M4/M1014

6 rounds

Magazine Capacity

The larger magazine capacity of the
light automatic weapons is offset by
their greater rate of fire and the fact
that it may take several bullets to
achieve the same effect as a single
shotgun shell. However, changing a
detachable magazine is much quicker
than reloading the internal tube
magazine of a traditional shotgun.

CHAPTER 5

Close Assault Weapons 2

Weight

▶ **Heckler & Koch MP5**
▶ **CZW 438 M9**
▶ **USAS-12**
▶ **Benelli M4/M1014**
▶ **FN P90**

Close assault weapons are normally used by specialist assault units, and by security forces optimized for short-range combat in an urban area. In both cases, personnel need to be able to move quickly, and must be as little encumbered as possible by their equipment.

Heavy weapons are tiring to use, especially when making rapid movements between the rooms of a building and constantly changing the weapon's position. They are also slow to come onto target, which can be a crippling deficiency in a situation where a threat may suddenly appear at close range, from an unexpected angle or from cover.

Submachine guns and personal defense weapons, firing small-caliber ammunition, tend to be very light but may require several rounds to put down a target that might be instantly disabled by a shotgun shell. Conversely, shotguns must, of necessity, be robust, which requires a fairly heavy construction. To this must be added the weight of ammunition – shotshells weigh much more than pistol cartridges, and while this is offset by a smaller capacity in traditional shotguns, weapons such as the USAS-12 carry a lot of weight in their drum magazines.

Spare drums are also bulky to carry and heavy, limiting the amount of ammunition that can be carried into action. Given the lethality of a fully automatic shotgun, this may not be too much of a drawback. Indeed, though ammunition capacity may be an issue for any close assault weapon, the question of how much can be carried by the user is less of a problem.

Protracted firefights are uncommon in a close-assault situation: fighting is intense and lethal, and tends to be over very quickly. How much ammunition is in the weapon is more of a consideration than how many spare magazines are carried.

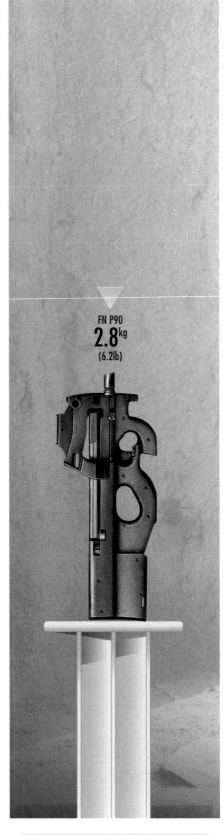

FN P90
2.8kg
(6.2lb)

kg
2.80

FN P90

CZW 438 M9
2.7kg
(6lb)

kg
2.70

CZW 438 M9

H&K MP5

3.08kg
(6.8lb)

Benelli M4/M1014

3.8kg
(8.4lb)

USAS-12

5.5kg
(12.1lb)

Weight

Modern lightweight materials have made it possible to create lighter weapons than previously, but there are some components such as the barrel and firing mechanism that still have to be made from high-quality steel. There is thus a practical limit to how light a weapon can be made.

	kg
	3.08

H&K MP5

	kg
	3.80

Benelli M4/M1014

	kg
	5.50

USAS-12

Muzzle Velocity

The amount of harm done by a bullet depends on its kinetic energy, which is determined by its mass and the square of its velocity. High velocity is thus a critical factor, but a certain amount of mass is needed for a round to remain effective.

948m/sec
(3,110ft/sec)

940m/sec
(3,084ft/sec)

930m/sec
(3,051ft/sec)

900m/sec
(2,953ft/sec)

884m/sec
(2,900ft/sec)

CHAPTER 6

Assault Rifles 1

Muzzle Velocity

▶ **M16A4**
▶ **L85A2**
▶ **QBZ-03**
▶ **AK-107/108**
▶ **Colt M4 Carbine**

M16A4

L85A2

QBZ-03

AK-107/108

Colt M4 Carbine

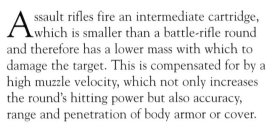

Assault rifles fire an intermediate cartridge, which is smaller than a battle-rifle round and therefore has a lower mass with which to damage the target. This is compensated for by a high muzzle velocity, which not only increases the round's hitting power but also accuracy, range and penetration of body armor or cover.

A high muzzle velocity allows the weapon to be fired in a very flat trajectory, enabling the user to point-and-shoot at ranges where accuracy with some weapons would require using and adjusting the sights. A high-velocity round also reduces the distance a moving target can travel between trigger pull and impact, which further contributes to the likelihood of a hit.

Assault-rifle ammunition tends to be similar the world over. The M16A4, M4 carbine and L85A2 all fire the standard NATO 5.56x45mm (0.219x1.8in) cartridge, while the Chinese QBZ-03 uses a marginally larger and heavier 5.8x42mm (0.228x1.65in) round. The AK-107 uses a lighter 5.45x39mm (0.215x1.54in) round, while the AK-108 variant uses NATO-compatible ammunition. The performance of these various rounds is remarkably similar in a combat scenario.

The muzzle velocity achieved by a weapon is determined by the amount of propellant in the cartridge, the weight of the bullet and the length of the barrel it is fired through. A light bullet accelerates faster than a heavy one, and a long barrel increases the time during which the bullet is being pushed by expanding propellant gases, i.e., the time during which it accelerates. Thus the M16A4 and the M4, which fire the same round, achieve a significantly different muzzle velocity.

OPPOSITE: This US infantryman is armed with an M4 carbine, which has replaced the M16 as the standard US longarm in recent years. The M4 has an effective range of 400m (437yd) and is fitted with a 30-round box magazine.

CHAPTER 7

Assault Rifles 2

Rate of Fire

▶ **M16A4**
▶ **L85A2**
▶ **QBZ-03**
▶ **AK-107/108**
▶ **Colt M4 Carbine**

QBZ-03

The assault rifle emerged as a result of experience in World War II, when urban and mechanized combat became increasingly prevalent. Troops moving in and out of vehicles need a light, short weapon that requires less room to maneuver. The same applies to personnel engaged in urban operations. Long-range accuracy is less useful than the ability to lay down withering firepower in response to a threat that emerges suddenly at close range. A lightweight weapon can be brought into action quickly and need only be accurate out to 300–400m (328–437yd). Combat beyond this range is unlikely.

M16A4

Rate of fire is extremely important in this sort of combat, as it increases the chance of hitting a hostile with enough rounds to put him down before he can shoot back. A burst can be "walked" onto a target and multiple hits are far more likely to stop an opponent than a single one. Conversely, automatic fire can result in a prodigious expenditure of ammunition, and troops that spray bullets all over the countryside risk running short when it really counts.

Colt M4 Carbine

Automatic fire is hard to control, resulting in a lot of misses. The main problem is "muzzle climb," where recoil pushes the barrel up and away from the target. However, controlled, aimed bursts of automatic fire are extremely effective when limited to a particular target. A high rate of fire can be an advantage when attempting accurate burst fire, as it ensures that the whole burst leaves the weapon before it moves too far off target.

AK-107/108

OPPOSITE: A US Marine aims an M16A4 fitted with an M203 grenade launcher. The modern assault rifle is a mature weapons system that can be integrated with a range of accessories. Advanced sighting systems give the individual soldier a significant advantage at longer ranges, while an underbarrel grenade launcher gives the squad some indirect fire-support capability against well-dug-in targets.

L85A2

Rate of Fire

The assault rifle permits entire squads to lay down suppressing fire, where previously this was a job for support weapons. This makes fire-and-movement tactics more effective and less hazardous for the personnel involved.

100^{rpm} ▲

◀ **60**^{rpm}

◀ **45**^{rpm}

◀ **40**^{rpm}

◀ **40**^{rpm}

19

Rate of Fire

The theoretical rate of fire for a weapon is based on its cyclic rate – the speed with which it can chamber and fire rounds from its magazine. This takes no account of the time required to reload the magazine. The M16A4 has a cyclic rate of more than 700 rounds per minute, but on a semiautomatic setting it is more likely to achieve around 60 rounds per minute. A trained rifleman using the Garand can fire 16–24 aimed rounds per minute.

M1 Garand

M1 Garand
24 rpm

M16A4

M16A4
60 rpm

Effective Range

The M1 Garand is theoretically capable of shooting out to 3,200m (3500yd) according to some sources. Its effective range is more realistically stated as 400m (437yd), which is much farther than most soldiers can shoot accurately with iron sights.

M1 Garand Range
400m
(437yd)

M16A4 Range
800m
(875yd)

M1 Garand

M16A4

Muzzle Velocity

The high muzzle velocity of the M16A4's 5.56x45mm (0.219x1.8in) round is offset by its tendency to lose energy more quickly than the heavier 7.62x51mm (0.3x2in) round fired by the Garand.

853 m/sec
(2,799ft/sec)

M1 Garand

948 m/sec
(3,110ft/sec)

M16A4

CHAPTER 8

WWII versus Modern Infantry Rifles

Rate of Fire, Effective Range and Muzzle Velocity

▶ **M1 Garand**
▶ **M16A4**

I n the early years of the twentieth century, the standard infantry weapon was a bolt-action rifle accurate out to several hundred meters. Individual marksmanship and large numbers of riflemen offset a low rate of fire. The M1 Garand was the first semiautomatic rifle to be adopted by the US armed forces, and provided each infantryman with an enormous superiority over personnel armed with bolt-action weapons. Every bit as rugged and accurate as the standard rifles of the day, the Garand could shoot more rapidly and be quickly reloaded with a new en bloc clip of ammunition.

However, even semiautomatic weapons were at a disadvantage in urban terrain when they came up against hostiles armed with submachine guns. An intermediate-caliber weapon was needed, capable of engaging accurately at a respectable range but offering fully automatic firepower for a close-quarters engagement. The assault rifle came to dominate the battlefield, and led to today's M16A4 rifle.

In addition to fully automatic fire when needed, the M16A4 also has a vastly greater ammunition capacity than the M1, and its detachable magazine offers quicker reloading than the Garand's clip-loading system. Its chief advantage, perhaps, is its adaptability. The M16A4 can be quickly and easily fitted with a range of accessories, including advanced optical sights, a vertical foregrip, a grenade launcher, a tactical light or even a laser sight. Although not intrinsically part of the rifle, these accessories enable the user to tailor it to a variety of specialist applications, improving effectiveness in the chosen role while retaining all-round capability.

LEFT: At about 90 percent of the length and 80 percent of the weight of an M1 Garand (see above left), the M16A4 is handier and less tiring to carry. However, once accessories such as a telescopic sight are considered, the infantryman's load has not changed much in the decades since the M1 was phased out.

CHAPTER 9

Bullpup Assault Rifles 1

Effective Range and Magazine Capacity

▶ **FAMAS F1**

▶ **QBZ-95**

▶ **SAR-21**

▶ **FN F2000**

▶ **IMI Tavor TAR21**

A "bullpup" rifle has the feed mechanism behind the trigger group rather than in front of it as a conventional rifle does. The magazine well and part of the action are located in the stock, making a folding stock impossible but greatly reducing the overall length of the weapon. This permits troops to carry a weapon that has the same accuracy as a full-sized rifle yet is short and handy. This is an advantage in urban combat or for mechanized troops who must mount and dismount from vehicles. The term "bullpup" may have been adopted from the name of an experimental post-World War II weapon, but whatever its origins it has come to apply to all weapons of this type.

The bullpup design did not become common until the late twentieth century, and has not supplanted the conventional rifle, as there are advantages to both traditional and bullpup configurations. The primary drawback with bullpup weapons is that they can only be fired from one shoulder (usually the right), due to the location of the ejection port. Certain designs, such as the FAMAS assault rifle and the Israeli Tavor TAR-21, overcome this by allowing the bolt and ejection port cover to be swapped, turning the weapon into a left-handed version.

The bullpup design is an evolution of the factors that gave rise to the assault rifle. Most combat takes place at ranges of less than 300m (328yd), so although long-range accuracy is useful at times, it is not the primary factor in assault-rifle design. For the typical infantry soldier, heavy firepower at a modest range is the most important feature of an assault rifle, backed up by reliability, ease of handling and lightness.

Magazine Capacity
A magazine capacity of about 30 rounds is the "industry standard" for most assault rifles. Indeed, many use standardized magazines based on those developed for the M16 family of rifles.

300m

FAMAS F1 Range
300ᵐ
(328yd)

25 x 5.56mm (0.219in) rounds

400m

QBZ-95 Range
400ᵐ
(437yd)

30 x 5.8mm (0.228in) rounds

SAR-21 Range
460ᵐ
(503yd)

30 x 5.56mm (0.219in) rounds

FN F2000 Range
500ᵐ
(547yd)

30 x 5.56mm (0.219in) rounds

IMI Tavor TAR21 Range
550ᵐ
(601yd)

30 x 5.56mm (0.219in) rounds

Effective Range

Although most combat is a matter of suppressive automatic fire or short-range point-and-shoot, the ability to accurately hit a target at several hundred meters remains a desirable feature in an infantry weapon.

L85A2

Muzzle Velocity

Minor differences in the construction of an assault rifle can cause variations in muzzle velocity. Chief among these is the length of the barrel. Within normal limits, a variation of a few meters per second will not greatly affect the accuracy or hitting power of a bullet.

940m/sec
(3,084ft/sec)

IMI Tavor TAR21

910m/sec
(2,986ft/sec)

FN F2000

900m/sec
(2,953ft/sec)

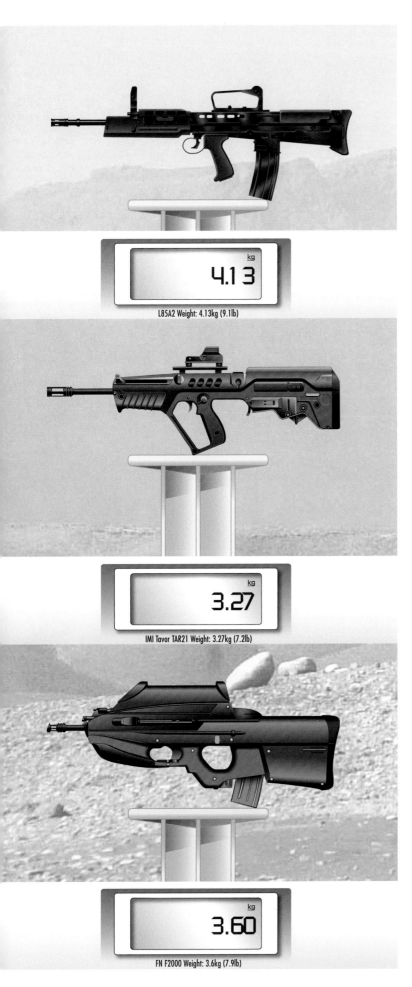

L85A2 Weight: 4.13kg (9.1lb)

IMI Tavor TAR21 Weight: 3.27kg (7.2lb)

FN F2000 Weight: 3.6kg (7.9lb)

CHAPTER 10

Bullpup Assault Rifles 2

Muzzle Velocity and Weight

► **L85A2**
► **FN F2000**
► **IMI Tavor TAR21**

The modern bullpup assault rifle, despite its futuristic appearance, represents an evolution rather than a revolution in weapon design. Plastic and lightweight alloys began to replace traditional steel and wood as early as the 1960s, though early attempts at plastic components could be brittle in cold conditions. The earliest bullpup assault rifle to be widely adopted, the Steyr AUG, entered service in 1979 and rapidly proved itself as a reliable and robust infantry weapon. With the concept proven, further development was assured and led to today's advanced rifles.

These weapons differ from previous generations of infantry rifles in more ways than their configuration. Construction uses advanced, strong but weight-saving materials that create a robust but lightweight weapon, and many rifles are designed either with a built-in optical sight or the capacity to fit one easily.

Such devices permit faster target acquisition and more accurate shooting than traditional iron sights. The design process uses modern ergonomic research, resulting in a weapon that is well balanced and easy to use under the stress of combat.

However, no weapon is better than its ammunition permits it to be, and most bullpup rifles are built around cartridges that have been in service for decades. This is largely dictated by logistical considerations: a change to a new ammunition type would be expensive and wasteful of existing stockpiles. There are weapons that use new cartridges, some with an extremely high muzzle velocity, but most mainstream rifles are built around existing ammunition such as the NATO standard 5.56x45mm (0.219x1.8in) round.

Weight

An assault rifle is inevitably going to be a fairly heavy piece of kit, especially once the weight of ammunition is considered. Modern weapons are constructed of lightweight materials to reduce weight, but one of the chief advantages of a bullpup weapon is the balance point, lying close to the user's body, which makes the weapon feel lighter than it actually is.

Conventional Assault Rifles 1

Effective Range and Caliber

- ▶ **AN-94**
- ▶ **INSAS**
- ▶ **FX-05 Xiuhcoatl**
- ▶ **Heckler & Koch G36**

The conventional assault rifle was not displaced by bullpup weapons. Indeed, many users find that a conventional layout offers more advantages than a bullpup, and have retained an existing design. In some cases, this is due to the evolution of an existing weapons system. For example, the US armed forces use variants of the M16 family, and the M4 carbine that is derived from it, and prefer to create ever more advanced variants of a proven weapons system than to replace it with an entirely new weapon.

The Heckler & Koch G36 and the visually similar FX-05 Xiuhcoatl drew on concepts used in previous generations of assault rifles, combining proven systems with new materials to create an advanced version of the traditional rifle. The INSAS was derived from the immensely successful Russian AK series of weapons, and incorporated concepts from other weapons including the FN FAL, which it replaced in service. It is chambered for NATO standard 5.56x45mm (0.219x1.8in) ammunition, which has become the standard assault-rifle cartridge in much of the world.

Conversely the AN-94, which was intended to become the new Russian service weapon, was built around the 5.45x39mm (0.215x1.54in) round and magazines used by the existing AK-74 but is a highly innovative design. Among its features is the ability to deliver a two-round "burst" at an incredibly high cyclic rate, effectively putting out two bullets instead of one. This is intended to aid penetration and stopping power without affecting accuracy. The weapon is also capable of more conventional automatic fire.

Effective Range

Effective range is, to a great extent, a theoretical concept. The weapon itself might be able to put a bullet where it is aimed at several hundred meters, but other than in the hands of a highly trained marksman this will not be achieved. It is a very rare soldier who can shoot accurately at his weapon's theoretical maximum range.

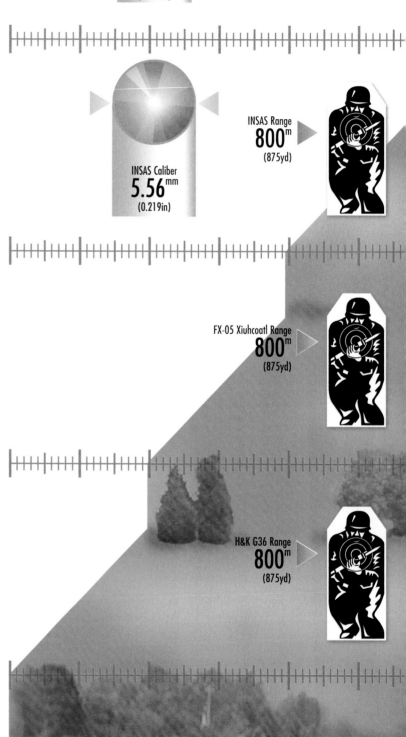

Caliber

The traditional 5.56x45mm (0.219x1.8in) and 5.45x39mm (0.215x1.54in) rounds have proved themselves a satisfactory balance of lightness, accuracy and stopping power at the ranges where an assault rifle is effective. Heavier and lighter rounds have been put forward, but have never achieved widespread popularity.

AN-94 Caliber
5.45mm
(0.215in)

INSAS Caliber
5.56mm
(0.219in)

INSAS Range
800m
(875yd)

FX-05 Xiuhcoatl Range
800m
(875yd)

H&K G36 Range
800m
(875yd)

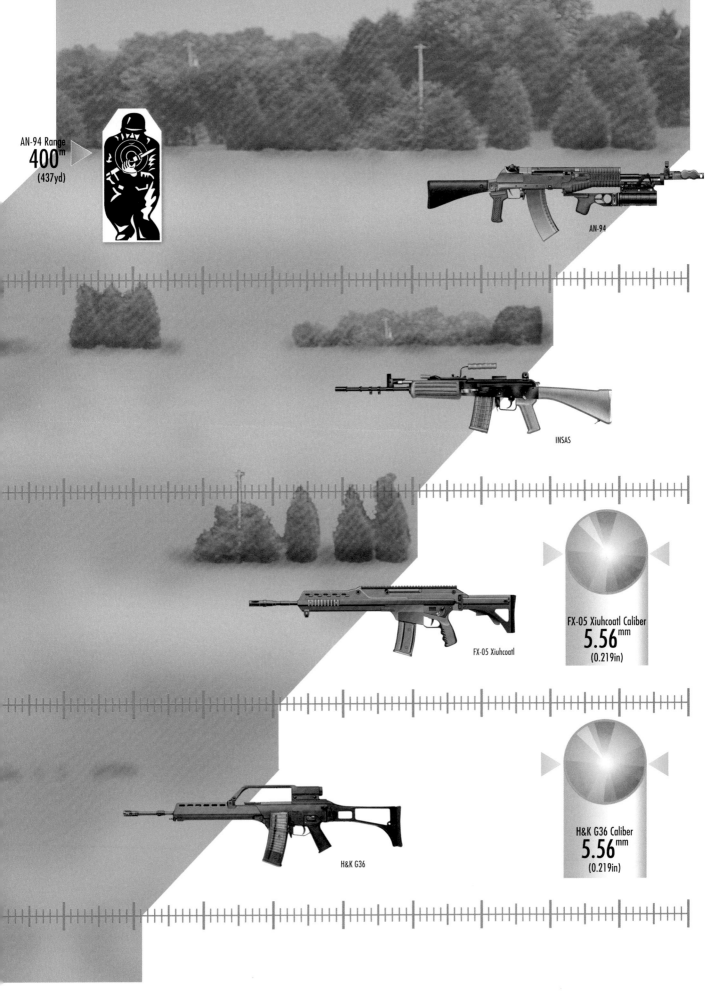

AN-94

INSAS

FX-05 Xiuhcoatl

FX-05 Xiuhcoatl Caliber
5.56ᵐᵐ
(0.219in)

H&K G36

H&K G36 Caliber
5.56ᵐᵐ
(0.219in)

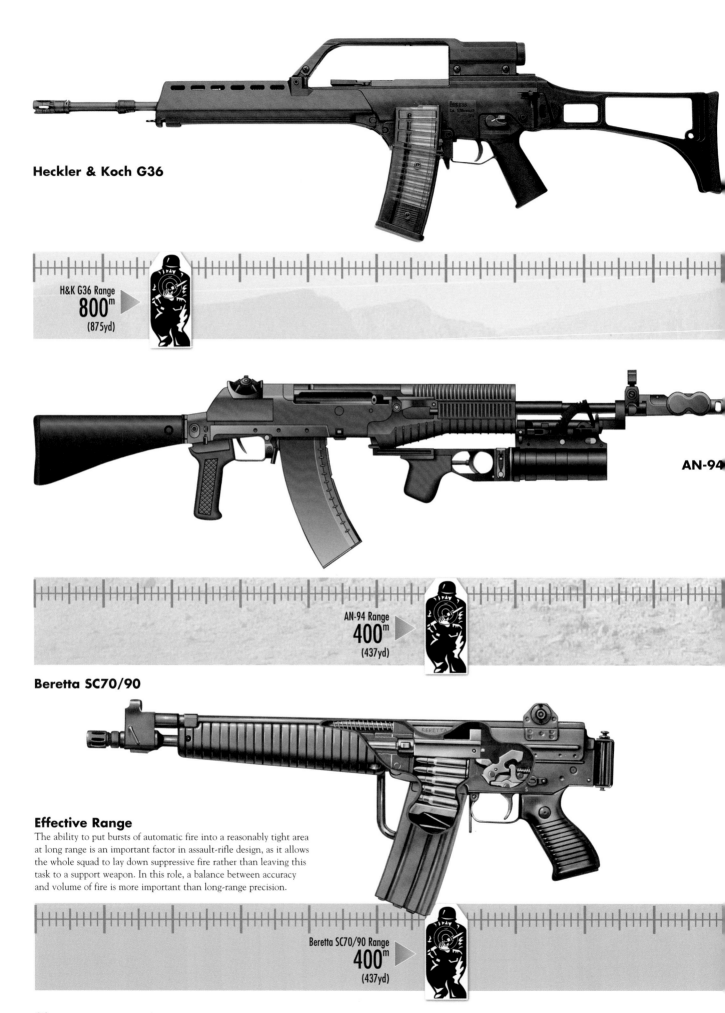

Heckler & Koch G36

H&K G36 Range
800ᵐ
(875yd)

AN-94

AN-94 Range
400ᵐ
(437yd)

Beretta SC70/90

Effective Range
The ability to put bursts of automatic fire into a reasonably tight area at long range is an important factor in assault-rifle design, as it allows the whole squad to lay down suppressive fire rather than leaving this task to a support weapon. In this role, a balance between accuracy and volume of fire is more important than long-range precision.

Beretta SC70/90 Range
400ᵐ
(437yd)

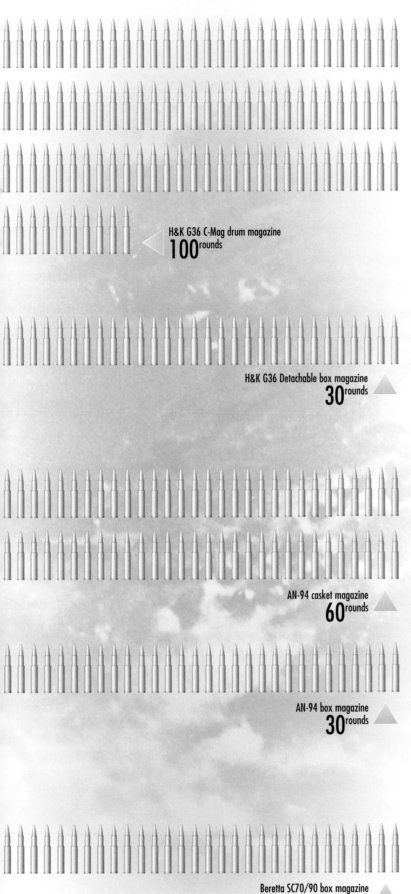

H&K G36 C-Mag drum magazine
100rounds

H&K G36 Detachable box magazine
30rounds

AN-94 casket magazine
60rounds

AN-94 box magazine
30rounds

Beretta SC70/90 box magazine
30rounds

300m

As a general rule, effective range is greater with larger-caliber weapons, though other factors such as the length of the weapon's barrel also affect performance over long distances.

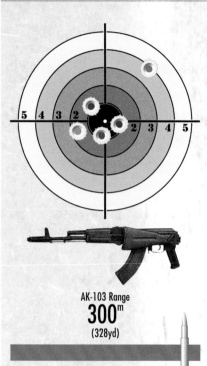

AK-103 Range
300ᵐ
(328yd)

400m

AICW Range
500ᵐ
(547yd)

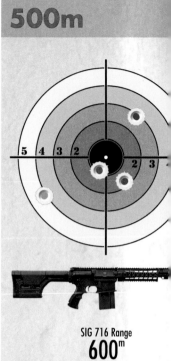

500m

SIG 716 Range
600ᵐ
(656yd)

20 x 7.62mm (0.3in) rounds

Magazine Capacity

The downside of using larger-caliber ammunition is additional weight and size, which may lead to a reduced ammunition capacity.

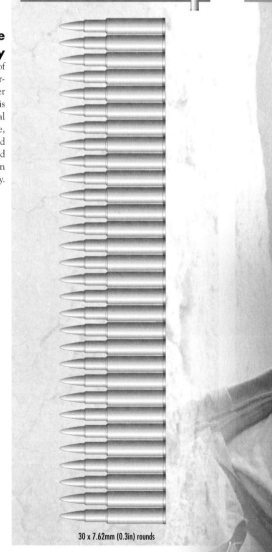

30 x 7.62mm (0.3in) rounds

30 x 5.56mm (0.219in) rounds

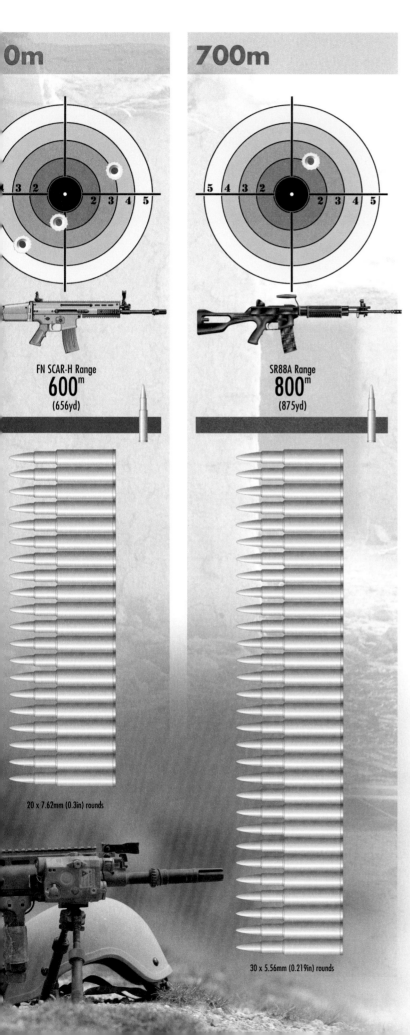

0m

700m

FN SCAR-H Range
600ᵐ
(656yd)

SR88A Range
800ᵐ
(875yd)

20 x 7.62mm (0.3in) rounds

30 x 5.56mm (0.219in) rounds

CHAPTER 13

Conventional Assault Rifles 3

Effective Range and Magazine Capacity

▶ **AK-103**
▶ **AICW**
▶ **SIG 716**
▶ **FN SCAR-H**
▶ **SR88A**

The requirements of modern infantry and special-operations units are always changing, and weapons developed to meet the needs of a previous generation may not always be appropriate to the current situation. Experience during and since World War II showed that an intermediate-caliber assault rifle was ideal for most combat situations, and that most combat troops did not need to engage at long range other than with suppressing fire. Recent experience in Afghanistan and other theaters has challenged this, and there is a current need for accurate fire at longer ranges.

Thus there has been a move back toward the heavier "battle-rifle" cartridge, which retains its energy and resists wind effects better than an intermediate-caliber round at longer ranges. The AK-103 returns to the original 7.62x39mm (0.3x1.54in) round used by its ancestor, the AK-47, while advanced Western rifles such as the SIG 716 and SCAR-H use the 7.62x51mm (0.3x2in) round favored for general-purpose machine guns and many sniper rifles.

This move is by no means universal. Advanced weapons such as the Australian Advanced Infantry Combat Weapon use the intermediate 5.56mm (0.219in) round, not least to reduce the weight of a weapons system that has two barrels, firing mechanisms and feed devices. Many armed forces continue to make exclusive use of 5.56mm (0.219in) weapons for their infantry, though environmental factors make it highly unlikely that a typical solider can shoot accurately at even half of the weapon's theoretical effective range.

OPPOSITE: A US Navy SEAL aims an FN SCAR-H assault rifle somewhere in Afghanistan, 2010. Introduced in 2009, the Special Operations Combat Assault Rifle (SCAR) is a modular system that includes a sniper rifle, close-quarters-battle rifle and grenade launcher. It has been adopted by many special forces, including those of the US military.

Effective Range

Sniping weapons have a lot in common with top-end hunting rifles, but hunters rarely shoot at the extremely long distances expected of a military sniper. Achieving a single-shot kill at several hundred meters requires a specialist weapon and an equally rare marksman.

Sako TRG22 Range
1,100ᵐ
(1,203yd)

SIG SSG3000 Range
1,000ᵐ
(1,094yd)

L96A1 Range
1,000ᵐ
(1,094yd)

SIG SSG3000

L96A1

Sako TRG22

5 x 7.62mm (0.3in) rounds

10 x 7.62mm (0.3in) rounds

10 x 7.62mm (0.3in) rounds

CHAPTER 14

Bolt-action Sniper Rifles

Effective Range and Magazine Capacity

▶ **SIG SSG3000**
▶ **L96A1**
▶ **Sako TRG22**
▶ **Steyr HS .50**
▶ **L115A3**

Opinion is divided on the relative merits of bolt-action and semiautomatic sniper rifles. Although semiautomatics offer faster follow-up shots and are more useful if the sniper team becomes involved in a close-range contact, bolt-action weapons have the advantage that they do not eject brass until the action is worked, which aids concealment. Bolt-action weapons are also slightly more accurate at long range, as there is no movement of internal parts until the bullet is long gone.

Sniping weapons are made to an extremely high standard and are accurate out to far greater ranges than ordinary rifles. They will send a bullet farther than their listed effective range, but at such great distances there will be considerable variation in the point of impact even if the weapon is kept perfectly steady, so sniping beyond the weapon's effective range is a matter of luck as well as skill. Very large-caliber weapons such as the HS .50 and L115A3 can achieve a greater effective range by a combination of heavy bullet and high velocity, but there is an upper limit to how powerful a rifle can be and remain portable by a sniper team.

For most applications, a 7.62x51mm (0.3x2in) round is entirely adequate, though specialist "match-grade" ammunition is preferred as it has the least variation between individual cartridges. A miniscule imperfection may not be very relevant at 100m (109yd), but in a 1,000m (1,094yd) shot it can cause significant deviation from the expected flight path and therefore a miss. The flight time of a bullet at long range is sufficiently long that many targets will be out of sight before a second shot can be taken.

HS .50 Range
500ᵐ
(1,640yd)

L115A3 Range
1,500ᵐ
(1,640yd)

Magazine Capacity
Bolt-action sniper rifles tend not to have a large magazine capacity, and in general one is not needed. A sniper will generally take at most three or four extremely precise shots before his target takes cover or is downed. In any situation where the sniper needs a greater ammunition capacity, he is using the wrong weapon entirely and is probably in serious danger.

Steyr HS .50

L115A3

1 x 12.7mm (0.5in) round

5 x 8.58mm (0.338in) rounds

OPPOSITE, TOP: Wearing the standard desert combat-dress uniform, a British infantryman aims an L96A1 sniper rifle.

CHAPTER 15

Semiautomatic Sniper Rifles

Weight

▶ **L129A1**
▶ **Dragunov SVD**
▶ **Stoner SR-25**
▶ **M14 Enhanced Battle Rifle**
▶ **M110**

Modern semiautomatic weapons are only slightly less intrinsically accurate than bolt-action equivalents, and at medium ranges this may not affect the shot significantly. There are times when a sniper may have the opportunity to engage several targets in rapid succession, and for such situations a semiautomatic weapon with a high magazine capacity offers very significant advantages. Semiautomatic weapons of this sort are often issued to designated marksmen, who are not fully trained snipers but infantrymen trained and equipped for long-range shooting. The presence of a specialist marksman and his weapon provides an infantry unit with the means to hit back at distant hostiles.

L129A1
4.5kg
(9.9lb)

kg
4.50

L129A1

Dragunov
4.68
(10.3lb)

kg
4.68

Dragunov SVD

Stoner SR-25
4.88^{kg}
(10.8lb)

M14 Enhanced
Battle Rifle
5.1^{kg}
(11.2lb)

M110
6.94^{kg}
(15.3lb)

Weight

A sniping weapon must be robust enough to retain its accuracy despite the inevitable knocks it will receive while in the field. This requires a fairly heavy weapon to start with, on top of which the sniper must also carry a range of specialist equipment including camouflage and vision devices.

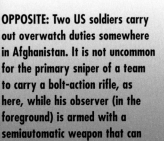

Stoner SR-25

M14 Enhanced Battle Rifle

M110

OPPOSITE: Two US soldiers carry out overwatch duties somewhere in Afghanistan. It is not uncommon for the primary sniper of a team to carry a bolt-action rifle, as here, while his observer (in the foreground) is armed with a semiautomatic weapon that can be used for both sniping and short-range firepower.

1 An Afghan Army marksman aims a Dragunov SVD rifle.

35

CHAPTER 16

Anti-materiel Rifles

Effective Range and Magazine Capacity

▶ **McMillan TAC-50**
▶ **Accuracy International AS-50**
▶ **Barrett M82A1**
▶ **Harris M87R**
▶ **Gerard M6**

The original anti-materiel rifles were created in World War I as a response to tanks, and though advances in armor protection soon rendered them ineffective, the concept of a powerful rifle capable of destroying hard targets remained viable. Today's anti-materiel rifles are sophisticated long-range weapons that can, in many cases, deliver specialist ammunitions such as explosive or armor-piercing rounds.

Anti-materiel weapons are intended for use on high-value equipment such as radar and communications sets, and are used by some law-enforcement agencies to disable fleeing vehicles. The US Coast Guard uses powerful 12.7mm (0.5in) rifles to cripple the engines of suspected drug-running boats that refuse to stop.

BELOW: A US Army sniper team uses an M82A1 anti-materiel rifle. Large-caliber weapons can be used for extremely long-range sniping and counter-sniping operations, or to eliminate key enemy personnel such as artillery observers and commanders who venture a little too close to the battle area.

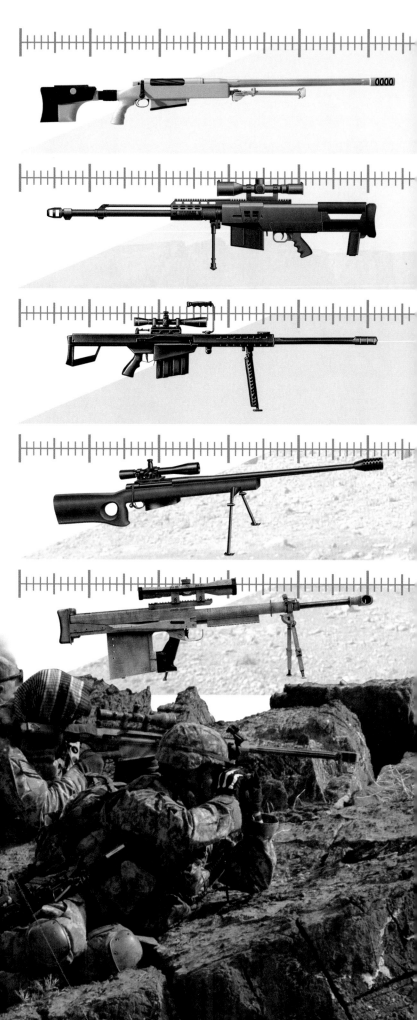

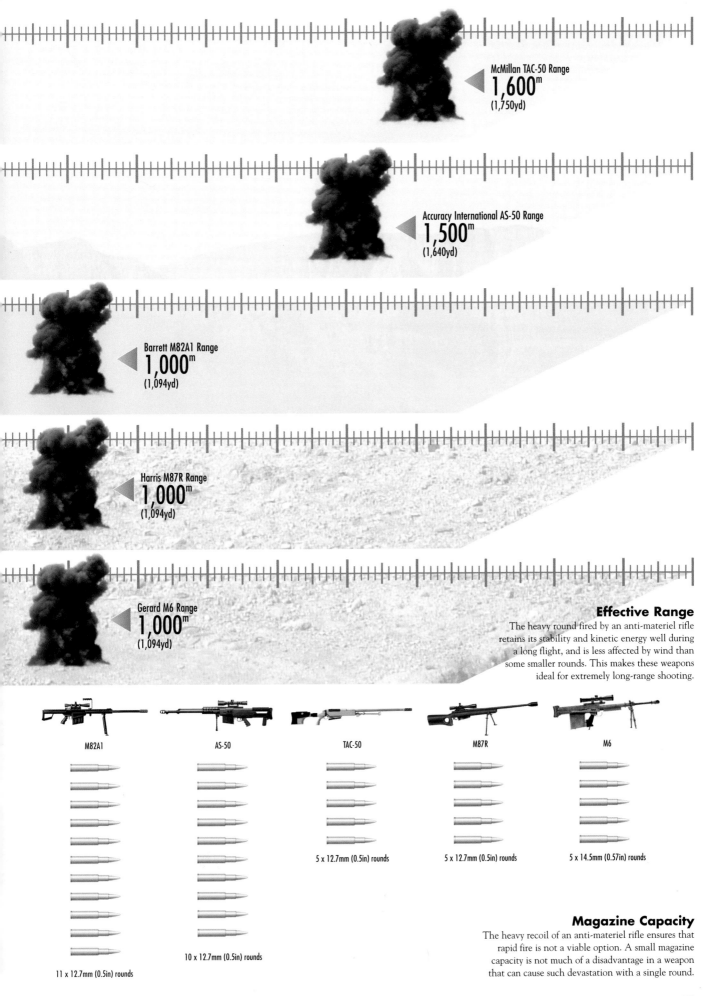

McMillan TAC-50 Range
1,600ᵐ
(1,750yd)

Accuracy International AS-50 Range
1,500ᵐ
(1,640yd)

Barrett M82A1 Range
1,000ᵐ
(1,094yd)

Harris M87R Range
1,000ᵐ
(1,094yd)

Gerard M6 Range
1,000ᵐ
(1,094yd)

Effective Range

The heavy round fired by an anti-materiel rifle retains its stability and kinetic energy well during a long flight, and is less affected by wind than some smaller rounds. This makes these weapons ideal for extremely long-range shooting.

M82A1 · AS-50 · TAC-50 · M87R · M6

5 x 12.7mm (0.5in) rounds

5 x 12.7mm (0.5in) rounds

5 x 14.5mm (0.57in) rounds

10 x 12.7mm (0.5in) rounds

11 x 12.7mm (0.5in) rounds

Magazine Capacity

The heavy recoil of an anti-materiel rifle ensures that rapid fire is not a viable option. A small magazine capacity is not much of a disadvantage in a weapon that can cause such devastation with a single round.

One-second Burst Weight of Fire

A light support weapon allows an infantry squad to bring intense firepower to bear when it is needed. In a close-range engagement, the ability to get a lot of lead moving downrange fast is often more important than sustained-fire capability.

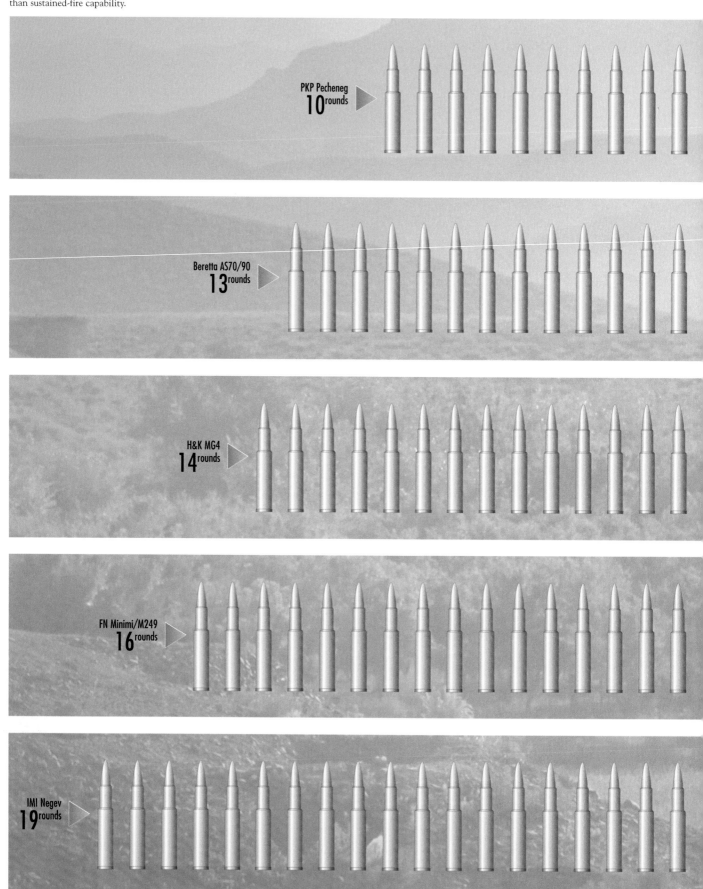

PKP Pecheneg
10 rounds

Beretta AS70/90
13 rounds

H&K MG4
14 rounds

FN Minimi/M249
16 rounds

IMI Negev
19 rounds

CHAPTER 17

Light Support Weapons 1

One-second Burst Weight of Fire

- ▶ **PKP Pecheneg**
- ▶ **Beretta AS70/90**
- ▶ **Heckler & Koch MG4**
- ▶ **FN Minimi/M249**
- ▶ **IMI Negev**

KP Pecheneg

Beretta AS70/90

H&K MG4

N Minimi/M249

IMI Negev

Light support weapons are intended to increase an infantry squad's firepower without reducing its mobility. Some are effectively overgrown assault rifles, while others are true machine guns with a quick-change barrel and large-capacity feed device. Light support weapons often lack the sustained firepower of a general-purpose machine gun, but they have the advantage of being integral to a squad and thus always available. Light support weapons are normally chambered for the same ammunition used by the rest of an infantry squad, and many can share magazines with riflemen if larger-capacity feed devices are not available. This creates an effective but lightweight weapons system that augments the squad's capabilities without imposing an increased logistics burden.

BELOW: The RPK-74 is simply an AK-74 rifle with a heavier barrel and larger magazine. It has served in the light-support role for decades but is being supplanted by more modern weapons, such as the PKP Pecheneg.

CHAPTER 18

Light Support Weapons 2

Effective Range

- ▶ **PKP Pecheneg**
- ▶ **Beretta AS70/90**
- ▶ **Heckler & Koch MG4**
- ▶ **FN Minimi/M249**
- ▶ **IMI Negev**

It is often possible to tell at a glance which design philosophy drove a given light support weapon's development. Those that were developed from general-purpose machine guns are usually belt-fed (though the belt may be carried in a box or drum) and have a quick-change barrel. These two factors greatly increase sustained-fire capability, as an overheated barrel can be changed and allowed to cool, and the weapon itself has the ammunition capacity to cause such overheating.

Light support weapons derived from assault-rifle designs have the advantage of commonality with the infantry squad's individual weapons. They are generally little more than an assault rifle with a heavier barrel to dissipate heat better, plus other accessories tailored to the machine-gun role. This simplifies logistics and maintenance, and permits any soldier to take over the weapon if its user is disabled. Another key advantage is the ability to share ammunition. Even if the light support weapon normally uses a drum or large-capacity box magazine, if it can take the same magazines as the rifle it was derived from, it can stay in action when its own ammunition supply is exhausted.

However, light support weapons tend to sacrifice range and sustained firepower for lightness and mobility. Assault-rifle-caliber light support weapons have an effective range that is little longer than that of a standard rifle.

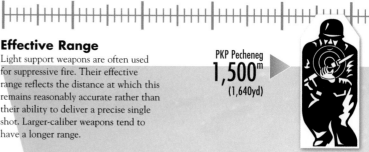

Effective Range

Light support weapons are often used for suppressive fire. Their effective range reflects the distance at which this remains reasonably accurate rather than their ability to deliver a precise single shot. Larger-caliber weapons tend to have a longer range.

PKP Pecheneg
1,500ᵐ
(1,640yd)

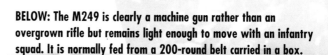

BELOW: The M249 is clearly a machine gun rather than an overgrown rifle but remains light enough to move with an infantry squad. It is normally fed from a 200-round belt carried in a box.

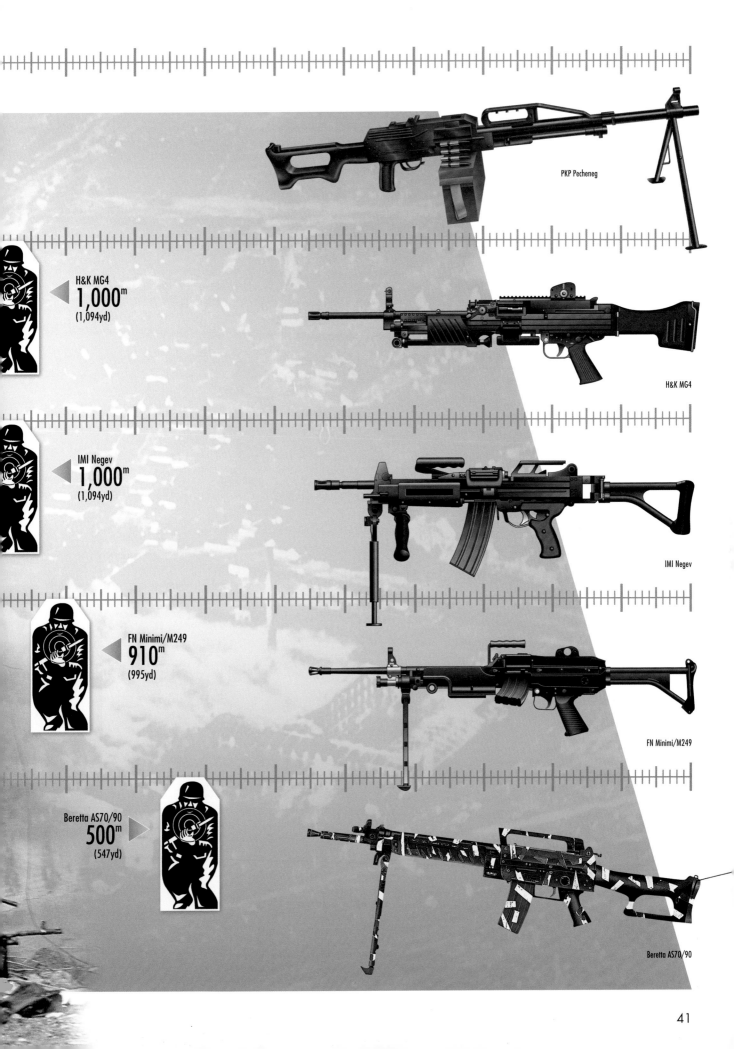

PKP Pecheneg

H&K MG4
1,000^m
(1,094yd)

H&K MG4

IMI Negev
1,000^m
(1,094yd)

IMI Negev

FN Minimi/M249
910^m
(995yd)

FN Minimi/M249

Beretta AS70/90
500^m
(547yd)

Beretta AS70/90

Effective Range

Most soldiers cannot shoot accurately at long distances under the stress of combat, so extremes of accuracy are wasted except in weapons intended for use by highly trained specialists.

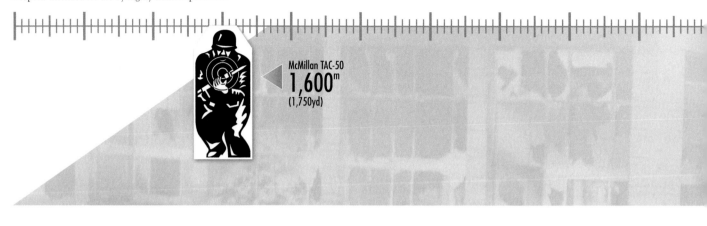

McMillan TAC-50
1,600^m
(1,750yd)

FN Minimi/M249
910^m
(995yd)

Colt M4 Carbine
600^m
(437yd)

LEFT: A US soldier practices on the firing range with an M4 carbine.

CHAPTER 19

Weapons Types Compared

Effective Range

▶ **McMillan TAC-50**
▶ **FN Minimi/M249**
▶ **Colt M4 Carbine**
▶ **Browning 9mm L9A1**

McMillan TAC-50
Used as a long-range sniper weapon
and anti-materiel rifle.

FN Minimi/M249
The standard squad-support light machine
gun used by most NATO forces.

Colt M4 Carbine
The primary longarm of the US
Army and effective up to ranges
of 400m (437yd).

Browning 9mm L9A1
50ᵐ
(55yd)

Browning 9mm L9A1
A popular handgun with various
NATO forces.

There is no such thing as a "best weapon"; each has a role to play and offers its user significant advantages in the right situation. A side arm such as the Browning L9A1 is useless at even fairly modest ranges, but there are circumstances where it is the only weapon that can be carried. A handgun leaves one hand free to open doors and undertake other tasks during room-clearance operations, and can be brought to bear in tight spaces. However, it is normally carried as a back-up or by personnel who do not expect to encounter the enemy directly.

The assault rifle and the squad automatic weapon (SAW) are the workhorse tools of the infantry soldier, offering a good balance of firepower and mobility. Their performance at all ranges is respectable, stopping power is acceptable and they will not slow down a squad's movement too much. The M4 carbine is a lightened and shortened assault rifle optimized for fairly close-range combat, in much the same way as the FN Minimi/M249 serves as a light fire-support platform. There are weapons with more hitting power or accuracy available, but these tend to be heavier, which may be a disadvantage in a combat environment where mobility and a rapid response time is critical.

Specialist tools such as anti-materiel rifles – for example the TAC-50 – are sometimes the only ones that can get a certain job done. However, they are bulky and heavy, and while the stopping power of a squad armed with 12.7mm (0.5in) rifles would be incredible, these weapons are simply not suited to highly fluid combat conditions.

Weapons Types

Infantry weaponry has evolved to suit the needs of modern combat, which typically takes place at ranges of at most 300m (328yd). The average infantry soldier needs a weapon that is most effective at this distance or less, where a few seconds of intense combat can be decisive. Long-range engagement is a task for specialists with precision weapons, or for an entire squad using automatic fire.

CHAPTER 20
Infantry Soldiers Compared

Weapons and Effective Range

▶ **US Infantryman**
▶ **Taliban Insurgent**

The equipment of combat personnel – be they highly trained regular soldiers or insurgent gunmen – tends to be surprisingly similar the world over. The assault rifle, in some form or another, has become the standard all-around infantry weapon. It offers a good balance of weight against firepower, effective range and ease of use. Assault rifles are also relatively cheap and easy to obtain, an important consideration when arming a large number of troops or militia fighters.

Taliban insurgents tend to be armed with weapons from the Soviet era, not least because large numbers of these weapons were obtained as a result of the Soviet involvement in Afghanistan in the 1980s. AK assault rifles in particular are very common on the international market – legally and otherwise – and are built under license or copied in small workshops worldwide.

The typical Taliban insurgent is lightly equipped other than his personal weapon, but stocks of support weapons such as RPD machine guns, SVD marksman rifles and the infamous RPG-7 are available.

Where support weapons are patchily available to some Taliban militia groups, the US military has a formal policy of ensuring that infantry are properly supported with squad automatic weapons, general-purpose machine guns and other heavy weapons, with additional support on call. In addition, the US infantryman's personal equipment includes vision aids, body armor and an array of useful tools. This level of support is a powerful force-multiplier that can enable US forces to defeat large numbers of gunmen whose weapons are, at first glance, apparently equivalent.

Effective Range

The capabilities of a weapon are less important than what a soldier can do with it. Properly supported by suppressing fire, an infantryman can move to a good position or take a carefully aimed shot, making best use of his weapon's capabilities, where an individual gunman may be forced to merely "spray and pray."

Beretta M9

Colt M4 Carbine

Colt M16

FN M24

FN M249

AK-4

RPD

Dragunov SV

RPG-

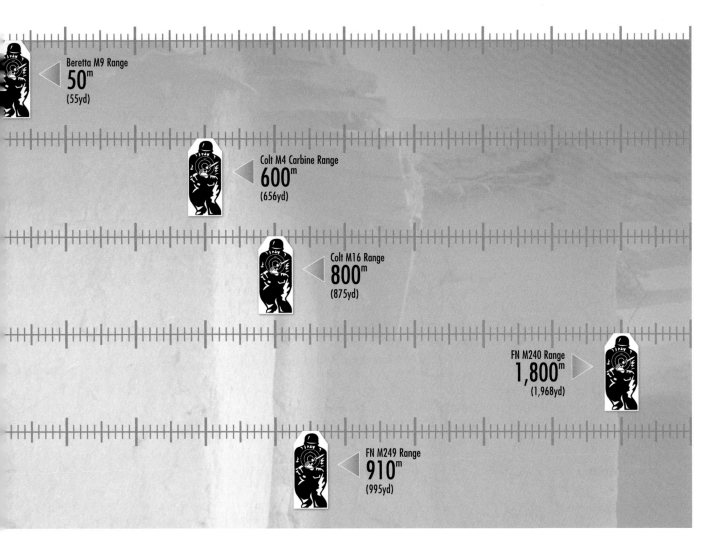

Beretta M9 Range
50^m
(55yd)

Colt M4 Carbine Range
600^m
(656yd)

Colt M16 Range
800^m
(875yd)

FN M240 Range
1,800^m
(1,968yd)

FN M249 Range
910^m
(995yd)

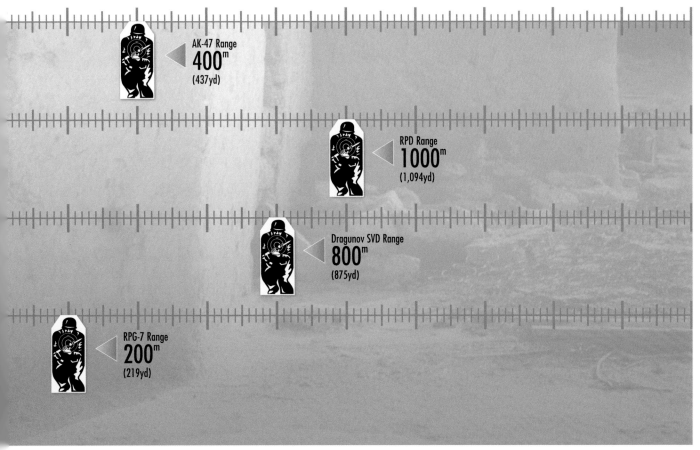

AK-47 Range
400^m
(437yd)

RPD Range
1000^m
(1,094yd)

Dragunov SVD Range
800^m
(875yd)

RPG-7 Range
200^m
(219yd)

45

Glossary

anti-materiel rifle A powerful rifle intended for attacking enemy equipment rather than personnel, such as radar or radio systems, vehicle and other military hardware.

automatic, fully automatic A weapon that will continue to load and fire as long as the trigger is held and ammunition is available, using the energy of firing each round to load the next.

ballistics A body of science connected with the behavior of projectiles.

bolt-action A bolt-action weapon may be a single-shot design, loaded directly into the chamber, or fed from a magazine. Either way, the spent case is not ejected until the bolt is manually worked. This makes it easy to collect spent cartridge cases but does not allow very rapid shooting.

bullet drop The effect of gravity on a bullet in flight will cause it to drop. Over a short distance this is insignificant but on a long shot, bullet drop must be compensated for or the round will fall short.

burst fire Firing an automatic weapon in controlled "bursts" of a few rounds is termed "burst fire." Some weapons are designed to be capable of firing a burst (usually three rounds) per pull of the trigger in the manner of an automatic weapon, then cutting off the burst until the trigger is released and pulled again.

designated marksman An infantry soldier trained to a high standard of accurate shooting and equipped with a precision rifle, but who lacks the advanced stealth and concealment skills of a fully trained sniper. Designated marksmen generally operate with and as part of an infantry force.

flash hider A short extension to the barrel of a weapon that conceals the "flash" of burning muzzle gases as they leave the barrel. A flash hider makes it much harder for hostiles to visually pinpoint a sniper's location by observing his muzzle flash, and also aids in night shooting by preserving the sniper's night vision.

lock time The delay between squeezing the trigger and the weapon actually discharging, a term derived from the firing mechanism of early firearms, known as a "lock"; e.g. flintlock, matchlock.

marksman A skilled and accurate shooter, or a holder of a formal shooting qualification at that level. Many police snipers could perhaps be more correctly termed marksmen as they lack the stealth and concealment skills of a military sniper, but by convention they are usually termed snipers.

muzzle brake A device by which some of the muzzle gases generated by firing a weapon are redirected in a direction that counteracts recoil and the tendency of the muzzle to rise. A muzzle brake makes a powerful weapon much more controllable.

muzzle energy The kinetic energy of a bullet as it leaves the weapon. Kinetic energy is a function of the velocity and mass of the bullet; greater muzzle energy equates to a shorter flight time, a flatter ballistic trajectory and greater wounding potential.

rifling Spiral grooves cut into the barrel of a weapon to spin the bullet as it passes. A spun bullet is gyroscopically stabilized and therefore much more accurate than otherwise. Any longarm that possesses a rifled barrel is technically a "rifle."

semi-automatic Also referred to as "self-loading," a semiautomatic weapon uses the energy of firing a round to eject the spent case and chamber the next. This may not always be desirable for a sniper, as spent cases may land outside his cover or attract attention as they reflect light. The internal workings of the weapon can also disrupt the aim point.

small arms Firearms light enough to be carried by infantry soldiers. The term is sometimes also loosely applied to support weapons such as man-portable anti-tank-missile launchers and machine guns, though this is technically incorrect.

smoothbore A non-rifled weapon such as a musket or shotgun, which fires a ball or group of pellets without imparting spin stabilization. Smoothbore weapons are inherently inaccurate and generally unsuitable for sniping, though a long barrel can somewhat compensate.

sniper The leader and main shooter of a sniper team, or a graduate of a formal sniper-training school. Also, a military marksman trained to observe and shoot from a concealed position. In popular usage, any person who uses a rifle from a concealed position.

suppressing fire High-intensity fire from small arms or support weapons aimed at the general area of the target. Suppressing fire is mainly intended to force the enemy to seek cover instead of shooting back, though it can cause casualties.

suppressor A device designed to reduce the noise of a weapon being fired by trapping some of the muzzle gases. It is not possible to completely "silence" a weapon; there will always be some sound upon firing. A more popular term is a "silencer."

trajectory The path followed by a bullet in flight, which will be a ballistic arc caused by the interaction of the projectile's muzzle energy, gravity and air resistance.

For More Information

Brady Campaign to Prevent Gun Violence (BCPGV)
1225 Eye Street NW, Suite 1100
Washington, DC 20005

(202) 898-0792
Web site: http://www.handguncontrol.org
The Brady Campaign to Prevent Gun Violence works to reform the gun industry by enacting and enforcing sensible regulations to reduce gun violence.

China Lake Museum Foundation
P.O. Box 217
Ridgecrest, CA 93556-0217
(760) 939-3530
Web site: http://www.chinalakemuseum.org
The China Lake Museum Foundation displays the navy's premier full-spectrum weapons research, development, and test facilities located in the Upper Mojave Desert at China Lake, California.

Military Channel
Discovery Communications, LLC
850 3rd Avenue, #1004
New York, NY 10022
(240) 662-3709
Web site: http://military.discovery.com/technology/weapons.html
The Military Channel is part of Discovery Communications, LLC, which airs a variety of programs on weapon technology.

National Rifle Association of America (NRA)
11250 Waples Mill Road
Fairfax, VA 22030
(800) 672-3888
Web site: http://www.nra.org
The NRA is America's foremost organization promoting gun rights and the Second Amendment.

Web Sites

Due to the changing nature of Internet links, Rosen Publishing has developed an online list of Web sites related to the subject of this book. This site is updated regularly. Please use this link to access the list:

http://www.rosenlinks.com/MODW/SArms

For Further Reading

Dougherty, Martin J. *Small Arms 1945-present*. London, England: Amber, 2012.
Dougherty, Martin J. *Small Arms Visual Encyclopedia*. London, England: Amber, 2011.
Fowler, Will, Anthony North, and Charles Stronge. *The World Encyclopedia of Pistols, Revolvers, and Submachine Guns*. London, England: Lorenz, 2007.
Fowler, Will. *Modern Weapons and Warfare: The Technology of War from 1700 to the Present Day*. London, England: Southwater, 2008.
Hartink, A. E. *The Complete Encyclopedia of Pistols and Revolvers*. Lisse, The Netherlands: Rebo, 2005.
Hogg, Ian V., and John Walter. *Pistols of the World*. Iola, WI: Krause, 2004.
Laemlein, Tom. *US Small Arms in World War II: A Photographic History of the Weapons in Action*. Oxford, England: Osprey, 2011.
The New Weapons of the World Encyclopedia: An International Encyclopedia from 5000 B.C. to the 21st Century. New York, NY: St Martin's Griffin, 2007.
Regan, Paula. *Weapon: A Visual History of Arms and Armor*. New York, NY: DK Publishing, 2010.
Rose, Alexander. *American Rifle: A Biography*. New York, NY: Delta Trade Paperbacks, 2009.

Index

A

Accuracy International AS-50, 36–37
Agram 2000, 9
AICW, 30–31
AK-103, 30–31
AK-107/108, 16–17, 18–19
AN-94, 26–27, 28–29
anti-materiel rifles, 36–37
assault rifles, 16–17, 18–19
      bullpup, 22–23, 24–25
      conventional, 26–27, 28–29,
        30–31

B

Barrett M82A1, 36–37
Benelli M4/M1014, 12–13, 14–15
Beretta AS70/90, 38–39, 40–41
Beretta SC70/90, 28–29
bolt-action sniper rifles, 32–33
Browning 9mm L9A1, 6–7, 42–43
bullpup assault rifles, 22–23, 24–25

C

close assault weapons, 12–13, 14–15
Colt M4 Carbine, 16–17, 18–19, 42–43
conventional assault rifles, 26–27,
      28–29, 30–31
CZW 438 M9, 12–13, 14–15

D

Dragunov SVD, 34–35

F

FAMAS F1, 22–23
FN F2000, 22–23, 24–25
FN Five-Seven, 6–7
FN Minimi/M249, 38–39, 40–41, 42–43
FN P90, 14–15
FN SCAR-H, 30–31
FX-05 Xiuhcoatl, 26–27

G

Gerard M6, 36–37

H

Harris M87R, 36–37
Heckler & Koch G36, 26–27, 28–29
Heckler & Koch MG4, 38–39, 40–41
Heckler & Koch MP5, 12–13, 14–15
Heckler & Koch MP5K, 9
Heckler & Koch MP7, 10–11
Heckler & Koch UMP, 10–11
Heckler & Koch USP, 6–7

I

IMI Negev, 38–39, 40–41
IMI Tavor TAR21, 22–23, 24–25
infantry rifles, WWII versus modern,
      20–21
infantry soldiers compared, 44–45
INSAS, 26–27

L

L85A2, 16–17, 18–19, 24–25
L96A1, 32–33
L115A3, 32–33
L129A1, 34–34
light support weapons, 38–39,
      40–41

M

M1 Garand, 20–21
M14 Enhanced Battle Rifle, 34–35
M16A4, 16–17, 18–19, 20–21
M110, 34–35
McMillan TAC-50, 36–37, 42–43

P

personal defense weapons, 9, 10–11
PKP Pecheneg, 38–39, 40–41
PMM, 6–7

Q

QBZ-03, 16–17, 18–19
QBZ-95, 22–23

R

Ruger MP-9, 9

S

Sako TRG22, 32–33
SAR-21, 22–23
semiautomatic sniper rifles,
      34–35
side arms, 6–7
SIG 716, 30–31
SIG P226, 6–7
SIG SSG3000, 32–33
small arms
      defined, 5
      weapons types compared,
        42–43
sniper rifles
      bolt-action, 32–33
      semiautomatic, 34–35
SR88A, 30–31
Steyr HS .50, 32–33
Steyr TMP, 9, 10–11
Stoner SR-25, 34–35

T

Taliban insurgent, compared to US
      infantryman, 44–45

U

USAS-12, 12–13, 14–15
US infantryman, compared to Taliban
      insurgent, 44–45

W

weapons types compared, 42–43

About the Author

Martin J. Dougherty is a writer and editor specializing in military and defense topics. He is an expert on asymmetric and non-conventional war. His published works deal with subjects ranging from naval weapons to personal security. He is the author of *Small Arms Visual Encyclopedia, Tanks World War II*, and *Essential Weapons Identification Guide: Small Arms: 1945–Present*.